Helping Hands
How to Help Someone Else Cope with Mental Health Problems

Tim Watkins

Life Surfing
Box 1 24, R&R Consulting Centre
41 St. Isan Road
Heath
Cardiff
CF1 4 4LW

www.life-surfing.com
info@life-surfing.com

ISBN 10: 1909093122
ISBN 13: 978-1-909093-12-6

Life Surfing is a community interest company limited by guarantee (07399335) registered in England and Wales.

Contents

Please Review This Book ! !

Thank you for Purchasing **Helping Hands** I am sure you will find it useful both to you and to those you care about. If **Helping Hands** was helpful to you, It will also be helpful to others. So please take the time to leave a review, so that you can help to help them too.

ABOUT THE AUTHOR

 Life Coach and Trainer, Tim Watkins is a founder-director of Life Surfing, a Cardiff-based community interest company established to help prevent mental illness and to promote wellbeing.

Tim Watkins graduated from Cardiff University with a first class honours degree in 1990.

Between 1990 and 1997 he worked as a policy research officer for the Welsh Consumer Council where he researched and wrote a range of policy reports including In Deep Water an investigation into problems in the aftermath of the North Wales ("Towyn") floods of 1990, and Quality of Life and Quality of Service an investigation into the promotion of quality of life in residential homes for older people.

Following a severe and enduring episode of depression between 1997 and 2000, Tim Watkins began working for the charity Depression Alliance, running its Wales office, and steering it to becoming an independent charity in its own right in 2005. He continued to run the charity (which re-launched as "Journeys" in 2007) until 2010. During that time, the Welsh Government appointed him to sit on the Health & Wellbeing Council for Wales and the Burrows-Greenwell Review of Mental Health in Wales. He also played a key role in developing the Healthy Minds at Work project, during which he wrote Taking Control, an audio self-help book for people affected by depression, and oversaw the development of the award-winning Depression Busting self-management programme for people affected by depression.

In October 2010, along with Julia Kaye and Paul Clarke, Tim Watkins formed Life Surfing CIC as a vehicle to address public wellbeing in people experiencing stress or whose life circumstances put them at risk of developing mental illness and people experiencing mild/moderate common mental illnesses such as anxiety and depression.

Tim Watkins, with Julia Kaye, has co-authored a range of training workshops:

- *How to Help in a Crisis*: a one-day workshop for people who want to learn how to help and support people with mental health problems
- *Distress to De-stress*: a 2 hour workshop for people who want to learn how to manage stress
- *Getting to Sleep*: a 2 hour workshop for people experiencing stress-related sleep problems
- *Banish your Blues*: a one-day workshop for people who want to learn how to self-manage depression

Tim Watkins is also the author of:

- *The Hidden Epidemic: An examination of suicide in the UK*
- *Depression Workbook: 70 Self-help techniques for recovering from depression*
- *Beating Anxiety: A Guide to Managing and Overcoming Anxiety Disorders*
- *Food for Mood: A guide to healthy eating for mental health*
- *Depression: A guide to managing and overcoming depression*
- *Getting to sleep: A guide to overcoming stress-related sleep problems*
- *Distress to De-stress: Understanding and managing stress in everyday life*
- *How to Help: A guide to helping someone manage mental distress*

Tim Watkins is also the editor of *The Wave* magazine.

Foreword

Mental health problems are common, affecting perhaps a quarter of us every year. In spite of this, we remain largely ignorant about mental health and mental illness.

In fact, most people with mental health problems do not go on to develop mental illness. And of those who do, the majority only experience relatively short episodes.

The good news is that recovery is the norm. Sustained recovery can be rapid, but is often hindered by a lack of support, treatment and self-help.

So long as those affected by mental illness are prepared to work toward recovery, and provided those around them offer appropriate support and encouragement, there is no reason why they cannot go on to lead productive and meaningful lives in future.

The reasons why most people do not readily help those affected by mental illness are our own ignorance and the fear that *we might do the wrong thing*. The result is that many of us stand aside and do nothing, unaware that *doing nothing is the worst thing we can do*.

People struggling to come to terms with mental distress are bewildered not understanding what is happening to them, and desperate for an answer. Seeing those close to them—family, friends, colleagues and neighbours—apparently rejecting them and abandoning them to their fate simply adds to the psychological trauma of a condition that is going to take time and support to overcome.

Using Helping Hands will help you become a skilled helper. The information contained in this book will give you a good understanding of mental health and mental illness.

This book will also provide you with a grounding in self-help and self-management techniques that you can encourage others to take up.

By putting what you have read here into practice, you will be able to hasten the recovery of those you care about.

Tim Watkins—June 2012

Introduction

Despite the publication of volumes of text about mental illness, surprisingly little has been written about how to help people affected by mental health problems. This leaves millions of people every year without the full support of those who would otherwise be best placed to help: spouses, partners, relatives, neighbours, friends and colleagues.

This book begins to fill this gap.

It is my belief that if more people had the knowledge and skills to help, support and encourage, we could achieve so much more. We could prevent people who have problems going on to be people who have mental illnesses. Every year we could prevent tens of thousands of people with mental health problems losing their jobs, their relationships and their housing. We could free up precious specialist mental health services to focus on the people who need them most.

We could start to roll back the numbers of antidepressants we prescribe and the millions of sick days lost to the economy.

I believe that there are four key elements to becoming a skilled helper:
o   an understanding of mental wellbeing, and of the various ways this can be undermined in our day-to-day lives
o   an understanding of mental illness and of the different diagnoses you may encounter
o   the skills needed to provide appropriate encouragement and support
o   self-care and self-help skills.

Helping Hands deals with each of these subjects in turn. It begins by offering a model that will help you understand the complexity of wellbeing, before looking at the ways in which wellbeing can be undermined, and how mental health problems can develop.

In the second section, Helping Hands looks at mental illness. This will help you understand the meanings of the various diagnostic and medical terms you may have heard. It will also help you understand the needs of someone affected by mental illness.

Section three is where you come in. This part of Helping Hands sets out the skills required of a lay helper. Here you will learn the "dos" and "don'ts" of encouraging and supporting someone who is experiencing mental distress.

Finally, Helping Hands looks at your needs—you will not be able to help someone else if you cannot keep yourself well in the process. Helping someone with a mental illness can be physically, emotionally and mentally draining. If you are going to be successful, you will need to develop your own coping strategies. This section will help you recognise and meet your own needs.

Helping Hands is inevitably concise. Volumes have been written about each of the topics covered. On the other hand, the aim is not to teach you to be a counsellor, psychotherapist or doctor. Rather, Helping Hands gives you with sufficient information to provide appropriate support and encouragement to those around you with mental health problems.

Mental Wellbeing

Wellbeing is more than health, and significantly more than the absence of illness. It is about you as a whole person—not just a biological entity, but a human being functioning effectively in a complex global society.

Wellbeing includes physical and mental health. It also contains those things that give meaning to your life—relationships, families, recreation, community, occupation, activity, etc. Wellbeing is also influenced by wider "human rights" factors such as the state of the economy, the nature of the state that governs in the area where you live, the degree of social cohesion, the provision of public services and utilities, etc.

A useful metaphor for wellbeing is a person pushing a burden up a slope:

In this model of wellbeing, the beginning and end of the slope are the start and finish of our journey through life.

The slope has two features:

o   the gradient (steep or gentle)
o   the surface (firm or slippery).

The gradient of the slope relates to the widest factors over which neither individuals nor groups of individuals have influence. These include the natural environment, climate, the political system (e.g., democracy, monarchy, dictatorship, theocracy) the type of economy (e.g., capitalism) the state of the economy, etc.

As individuals we can do very little to directly influence the angle of the slope. We can, of course, rebel, protest, join political parties, and establish campaign groups, so that we can collectively alter the world we live in. However, from day to day, we usually have to accept that life has its ups and downs—sometimes the slope is gentle, other times it is steep.

The friction of the slope is about the institutions we live our lives through. An institution is not (as is often thought) a large building like a hospital or a bank. Rather, the term "institution" refers to the social relationships between groups of people. Often, institutions have unequal distribution of power and resources. Thus, a hospital is an institution because it is run by a powerful health board, managed by officers and doctors of various rank, and containing relatively powerless patients.

Less obvious "institutions" include neighbourhoods, families and social groups such as ramblers clubs—each has its (albeit informal) hierarchy and power dynamic.

A healthy institution is one that is nurturing and helps its members realise their full potential as human beings. In the model, this would be a high friction slope offering plenty of grip, and aiding your journey through life. An unhealthy institution is one that at best stifles its members, and at worst abuses them. This would be a low friction slope offering little or no grip, and making your journey through life all the harder.

The "burden" that we all carry through life is the person we are:

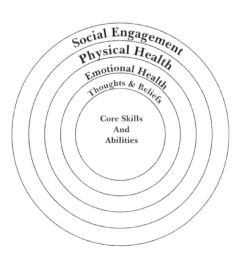

The outer edge is about how we operate in society—our social being. This varies from person to person. Some are extroverted, some introverted. Some enjoy spending time with large groups of people, others seek solitude. Some take risks, others play by the rules.

The next layer refers to our physical being. We have a body. It contains systems for breathing and digestion; it has various organs that keep us alive. It has skeleton, tendons, muscles and cartilage to help move us around. It has various senses that let us know what is going on around us. It has a brain that processes all of this information, and automatically adjusts the parts of the body.

No two bodies are the same—even identical twins have differences. But most differences (hair and eye colour, height, skin tone, etc), unless extreme, have little impact on wellbeing. However, some differences result from illness or disability, and can have a major impact on wellbeing.

Next is our emotional being. This relates to how "sensitive" we are. Some people are in touch with their emotions. Others are ruled by them. Someone prone to depression might have overly negative feelings about themselves and the world around them.

Next comes mind. This is about our thoughts and beliefs. Some people are "open minded" and flexible in their beliefs. Others are very rigid in what they think and believe about themselves, others and about the world around them.

At the centre of the model are our core skills and attributes. If you are a religious or spiritual person, you may think about this as to do with your "mission" or "dharma" - this is the idea that you come into the world with a purpose, and that to aid with this, you are born with core skills and attributes to enable you to realise your goals.

If you are not religious or spiritual, let us just note that people inherit genetic traits that make them better suited to some things than others. For example, someone born with perfect pitch coupled to strong and slender musician's fingers may be drawn to play music, while someone with an athlete's build and a degree of single-mindedness may excel as a sports player.

Put more simply, we all have things that "make us tick".

Either way, you will feel unhappy and dissatisfied with your life if your core skills and abilities are thwarted.

Finally, the person doing the pushing is the "I" (or in the language of Freud, the "ego") who sits at our centre, watching everything that is happening around and to us, and directing our responses.

Ideally, then, we seek to have a small burden to push along a gentle, firm slope. As individuals we can do some of the things needed to achieve this. We can develop our core skills and attributes, and bring our thoughts and beliefs, emotions, physical body and social being into harmony with them in order to fulfil our lives.

However, while we may wish for healthy institutions, we cannot deliver these alone—we must work with our relatives, friends, neighbours and colleagues to develop and sustain supportive, nurturing institutions.

Even this type of social solidarity (or "big society") can do little to influence the angle of the slope. Some elements of the slope, such as climate change, are beyond the control of nation states. States may collectively affect the global economy, but even this cannot prevent "boom and bust". Those of us lucky enough to live in democracies can vote for a change of government, and can protest between elections. But for the most part, we just have to bear those things that make for a steep slope.

It is important to understand that these wider factors have a much greater impact on wellbeing than do the actions we take as individuals. This, sadly, is born out in official health surveys that consistently find poor health and wellbeing in the poorer areas of the UK. This is true even where people in poorer areas lead healthy lifestyles, while people in affluent areas live unhealthily. A healthy person in an upper valleys town in South Wales has a lower life expectancy than a relatively unhealthy person in Kensington and Chelsea simply as a result of the prevailing economic conditions in those two communities. This will be compounded where institutions are unhealthy—something that is also less likely in more affluent communities.

While encouraging healthy lifestyles is important, we should avoid the tendency to blame people who become sick or disabled for their plight. The fact remains that while we must each strive for wellbeing, many of its elements are beyond our control.

The Mental Health Continuum

> *"Mental health influences how we think and feel about ourselves and others and how we interpret events. It affects our capacity to learn, to communicate, and to form, sustain and end relationships. It also influences our ability to cope with change, transition and life events—having a baby, moving house, experiencing bereavement."* (Lynne Freidli—mental health improvement briefing paper 2004)

One can imagine a scale of health that has illness at one end and good health at the other:

Illness  Health

We might put people with infectious illnesses such as measles or pneumonia, or conditions like angina or dementia to the left of the scale. We might them put athletes and people who work out to the right of the scale. The rest of us would cluster around the middle.

Mental health – or "wellbeing" – is different. A physically healthy person doesn't necessarily enjoy good mental health, while someone with a chronic illness such as diabetes or heart disease doesn't automatically have poor mental health.

Nor is this mismatch between diagnosis and mental health limited to people with physical illnesses and disabilities. A person with a diagnosis of a mental illness does not necessarily have poor mental health (although during an episode of their illness they will have).

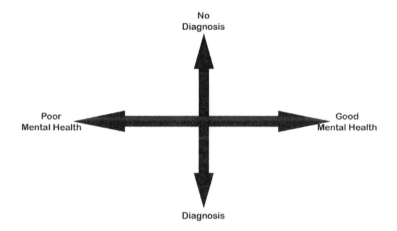

Someone with a diagnosis of depression, for example, may begin with no diagnosis but with poor (and deteriorating) mental health. If their mental health deteriorates to the point that they seek medical help, they will be diagnosed with depression.

With appropriate treatment, support and encouragement, their mental health will improve (although they still have their diagnosis). Eventually, they will recover, and move on with their life.

In fact, the majority of people who experience poor mental health never seek medical help and are never diagnosed with a mental illness. This is especially true of people with common conditions such as anxiety and depression, where only 20% of those affected are diagnosed (the remainder being able to recover using self-help strategies with the support of friends and relatives). While the majority of people with severe mental illnesses such as bipolar depression and schizophrenia do require medical support and on-going treatment, even within this group, around a third recover without medical support.

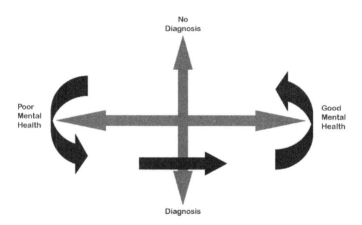

How common is mental illness?

Definitions of mental illness change every 10 years or so. Things that used to be mental illness (e.g., homosexuality) are reclassified. Meanwhile (and more often) ordinary human emotions and behaviours (e.g., shyness, grief, excessive drinking) are increasingly defined as mental illness. These changes make arriving at a definitive figure quite difficult. Moreover, a lack of clarity between "mental health problems" and "mental illness" tends to result in an over-estimation of the numbers.

Around 1 in 4 people in the UK report "having a problem with mental health" in any year. However, only 1 in 10 is diagnosed with a "mental illness" (even this may be an over-estimate where the same people have several episodes of illness in the same year).

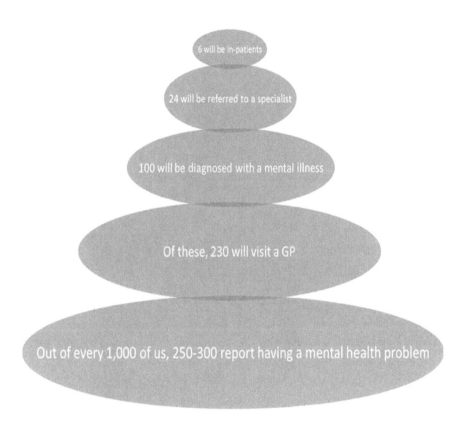

6 will be in-patients

24 will be referred to a specialist

100 will be diagnosed with a mental illness

Of these, 230 will visit a GP

Out of every 1,000 of us, 250-300 report having a mental health problem

Three quarters (76%) of those diagnosed with a mental illness will be treated solely in primary care with a combination of medication, counselling and self-help.

The remaining 24 percent will be seen by a Community Mental Health Team (CMHT) made up of psychiatrists, psychologists, nurses, occupational therapists and physiotherapists. The CMHT will provide a more focussed package of treatment and support.

Finally, six percent of those diagnosed with a mental illness will be admitted to an in-patient setting (a residential unit or a hospital bed). Less than one percent will be detained under the Mental Health Act.

Anxiety, depression, phobias, OCD and panic disorder are the most common mental illnesses. Psychosis (bipolar and schizophrenia) are rare, and are more prevalent in men. Significantly more women than men develop common mental illnesses.

Around 5,000 people in the UK take their own lives every year (about 320 people in Wales). This is almost double the numbers who die in road traffic accidents. The two factors most linked to suicide are mental illness and poverty. It is important to take suicide seriously.

Stress and mental illness

Often, common mental illnesses are related to stressful life events. This may be less so with psychosis, although stress is often a trigger for someone having a psychotic episode.

Stress is the result of our biological defence mechanisms coming into conflict with our social circumstances.

Our bodies are set up to respond to threats in one of three ways:

o   Fight

o   Flight

o   Freeze.

Each would have increased the chance of survival depending on the nature of the threat. However, in the modern world, they are not particularly useful. If your manager is hassling you to meet a deadline, freezing or fleeing aren't going to help, while fighting is going to get you fired (or worse).

Actually, a degree of stress is helpful as it can help focus the mind and increase physical performance. Unfortunately, there is only a small space between optimum performance and tipping into unhealthy stress. Moreover, if stress is prolonged, our resilience falls, and we tip into unhealthy stress much sooner.

If we experience unhealthy stress for a prolonged period, we are not only at risk of developing mental illness, but also a range of physical illnesses. Think about what you do to cope with stress. Do you:

o Use alcohol?

o Stay at home away from people?

o Smoke?

o Eat chocolate (or sweets)?

o Use coffee to stay awake?

The way we respond to short-term stress is usually also the way we try to cope with long-term stress. With the exception of smoking, these are reasonably good short-term responses. However, long-term use will serve to add illness to your stress, and will make it harder to cope.

Symptoms of stress-related illness include:

o **Brain & nerves**: headache, lack of energy, disrupted sleep, anxiety, problems with concentration and memory

o **Skin**: acne, eczema, rashes

o **Muscles & joints**: tension, pain, reduced bone density

o **Heart**: increased heart rate, raised blood pressure, higher cholesterol, increased risk of heart attack

o **Digestive system**: nausea, heartburn, diabetes, diarrhoea, constipation, pain

o **Immune system**: less ability to fight off or recover from infection

o **Reproductive system**: irregular and painful periods, impotence, lowered sperm count, loss of sex drive.

Healthy ways of coping with stress include:

o   Physical exercise

o   Massage

o   A soak in the bath

o   A healthy meal (especially with friends)

o   Yoga, tai chi or Pilates

o   Meditation.

Getting into healthy ways of de-stressing at times of short-term stress helps maintain the habit when faced with long-term stress.

When does stress become illness?

There are no objective tests for mental illness. Diagnosis is made on the basis of symptoms, duration and on the impact on someone's life. This latter is the most important.

Where someone is struggling to cope with day to day living, it is important that they receive help and support. They may be one of the 20 percent who cannot recover without medical help. And even if they aren't, soldiering on without help may cause recovery to take significantly longer than would otherwise have been the case.

The next section of the book looks at the symptoms and warning signs of the most common mental illnesses. It looks at how they are treated, and what people with these illnesses can do to help themselves. And it sets out what you can help and encourage them to do.

Mental Illness

Anxiety

Every one of us knows what anxiety is like. Just think about a time in your life when you had to face something stressful such as:

o a job interview

o an exam

o a driving test.

The chances are that you didn't sleep well the night before. Telling yourself that you needed sleep didn't help, so you tossed and turned into the early hours. When you woke up, you felt tired and irritable. Your stomach had butterflies. You may have felt that you wanted to use the toilet more often than you needed to.

The common symptoms of anxiety are:

o Unrealistic fear or worry

o Racing thoughts

o Poor concentration and memory

o Irritability and anger

o Disrupted sleep—not sleeping, early waking, tiredness

o Avoiding social situations

o Rapid heart beat

o Palpitations

o Rapid, shallow breathing

o Dizziness

o Tingling and numbness

o Muscle tension, aches, headache

o Stomach problems, diarrhoea

o Restlessness

o Urinary frequency

While many of us will have experienced several (or even most) of these symptoms at some time or another, they tend to be short-lived and related to a specific situation. When someone develops an anxiety disorder, the symptoms:

o   Usually occur without good reason
o   Last for considerably longer
o   Are so severe that they interfere with the person's ability to cope with daily living.

Anxiety disorders affect around 6% of the population at any time. There are several types:

o   Phobias
o   Generalised anxiety disorder
o   Panic disorder
o   Obsessive Compulsive Disorder
o   Traumatic Stress Disorders.

Phobias

Remember that anxiety disorders are not rational. If a person is terrified because they have come face to face with a burglar, their anxiety is entirely reasonable and understandable. When they experience a similar level of fear when confronted with, say, a money spider, we might reasonably say that they have arachnophobia.

Fear of spiders is common (although largely irrational if you live in the UK). In most cases, phobias do not qualify as anxiety disorders because they are not so strong as to interfere with people's ability to get on with their life. If, however, someone were so scared of encountering a spider that they refused to go out, then they could benefit from treatment and support to help them overcome their phobia. Phobias come in all shapes and sizes (remember they are irrational). The Phobia List website – www.phobialist.com – contains hundreds of entries.

Some phobias, such as agoraphobia (a fear of open spaces) and social phobia can be more disabling because they are more generalized – both fears can be realised the moment you step outside your front door.

Generalised Anxiety Disorder

Someone with a generalised anxiety disorder will experience all of the symptoms of fear, but without any particular thing to be afraid of. This fear can be overwhelming, and may tip over into panic.

Because anxiety disorders involve physical symptoms related to the body's "fight, flight or freeze" response, people with anxiety disorders may feel that there is something physically wrong with them. For example, rapid heart rate, palpitations and shortness of breath may be mistaken for a heart problem or heart attack. This can result in a state known as a "panic attack", in which the symptoms of anxiety spiral out of control.

Although panic attacks are harmless, and wear themselves out after 15-20 minutes, they are a thoroughly unpleasant experience to go through—especially for someone having an attack for the first time.

Panic Disorder

A panic disorder develops where someone who has been experiencing panic attacks seeks to control these by avoiding the situations and circumstances in which the panic attacks occur. For example, someone whose panic attacks seem to occur in supermarkets may avoid going to them, while someone whose panic attacks occur when using public transport may avoid travelling.

These responses help produce a downward spiral of anxiety because giving in to fear (by avoiding the triggers of fear) works to strengthen the fear.

One of the most common treatments for anxiety disorders is a process of "graded exposure" in which someone is supported and encouraged to gradually face their fears.

This process is most commonly seen with treatments for phobias. Several airlines used to run graded exposure courses for people afraid of flying. These would begin with looking at pictures and films of aeroplanes, together with lessons in how they fly and what the risks are. Next, participants would sit inside a plane on the ground. Eventually, they would take a flight around the airport.

Obsessive Compulsive Disorder

Although Obsessive Compulsive Disorder (OCD) is most obviously about irrational behaviours, it is an anxiety disorder because the behaviours are a response to underlying fears and anxiety.

Many of us will have experienced a small insight into obsessive behaviour—for example, you may have forgotten whether you locked your front door, and will either have returned home to check, or sat obsessing about it during the day. Alternatively, you may have had a "lucky charm" or a "lucky behaviour" that you had to use when faced with an important event or situation. Former England soccer captain David Beckham had a routine for putting his boots on to bring him luck on the field.

These examples are harmless enough, and, in the case of luck, may have a degree of truth in them insofar as someone who feels lucky may be more relaxed and "in the zone", and therefore more likely to succeed.

People with OCD experience significantly greater anxiety and a much greater degree of compulsion to behave in anxiety-relieving ways. So much so, that they are unable to get on with their lives.

Going home to check you locked the door is one thing. Being compelled to repeat this behaviour many times a day, or to the point that you dare not leave the house, is an altogether different matter.

OCD often develops in childhood. Without support, it can develop into a lifelong condition. So, as with all anxiety disorders, it is important to take them seriously.

Traumatic Stress Disorders

Traumatic stress disorders have a degree of rationality to them as they are connected to real events involving danger, violence, death and mutilation.

Where someone is involved in or a witness to a traumatic even, such as armed conflict, terrorist attack, man-made disaster, or road traffic accident, they are at risk of developing a stress disorder.

Symptoms of stress disorder include:

o   Psychic numbing (in which emotions cannot be experienced)
o   Withdrawal and avoidance
o   Increased arousal and vigilance (being on edge)
o   Unrest and unease in similar situations or circumstances
o   Re-living, intrusive memories and flashbacks.

An Acute Stress Disorder will manifest almost immediately after the event.

This makes diagnosis easier, although treatment, support and encouragement will be needed to help the person integrate their experience and move on with their life.

Post Traumatic Stress Disorder is where the symptoms of stress disorder begin months or even years after the event. This can make diagnosis more difficult. One reason why relatives, friends and colleagues can play a crucial role for this group is that they are likely to be aware of the trauma that the person experienced and can link the symptoms of anxiety to the traumatic experience.

Mixed Anxiety and Depression

Anxiety symptoms are not limited to anxiety disorders. The symptoms of anxiety can be part of the experience of people with any mental illness. Indeed, the most common mental illness is mixed anxiety and depression, which affects around 12 percent of us in any year.

Although most depressed people do not experience anxiety, a sizeable minority do. In some cases, the symptoms of depression and anxiety appear together. In other instances, prolonged anxiety symptoms cause an episode of depression.

Depression

Depression is a common condition affecting around 10 percent of us in any year. In most cases, people with depression are able to recover without needing formal medical treatment. However, in about 20 percent of cases, people become severely depressed. There is no way of knowing in advance who will recover and who will get worse.

As with anxiety, most of us will have an insight into depression from times in our lives when we have experienced profound emotional pain or loss. Stressors such as bereavement, separation and redundancy can impact heavily on us, leaving us with low mood and a sense of helplessness.

However, as with anxiety, the experience of depression is different because the symptoms:

o   Last for considerably longer, and
o   Are so severe that they interfere with the person's ability to cope with daily living.
o   The main symptoms of depression are:

- o   Sadness or low mood

- o   Tiredness or exhaustion

- o   Withdrawal, loss of interest and loss of pleasure or enjoyment

- o   Disrupted sleep

- o   Feelings of helplessness and hopelessness

- o   Guilt and low self-esteem

- o   Poor concentration and memory

- o   Loss of confidence.

It is worth remembering that although we all experience some of these symptoms at times in our lives, more than 80 percent of us will never experience depression to such severity that we would qualify for a diagnosis.

These days, depression is categorised by its severity as well as its symptoms. People with depression are divided into three groups based on the number, severity and duration of their symptoms:

- o   Mild depression has fewer symptoms and less of an impact on daily living

- o   Moderate depression has more symptoms and interferes with daily living

- o   Severe depression has most of the symptoms and prevents those affected from engaging in ordinary patterns of daily living. Severe depression may also involve a high risk of suicide.

The causes of depression are not clear. Several theories have been put forward. The most common are:

- o   Serotonin theory—depression is caused by low levels of a chemical (the neurotransmitter serotonin) in the brain

- o   Negative thoughts and beliefs—depression is caused by negative, unrealistic or unhelpful thoughts and beliefs.

Depression is more complex than these theories allow. It is most likely that low levels of neurotransmitters and negative thoughts and beliefs are caused by depression in the first instance (although they become reasons for depression persisting).

Most depression is reactive—it is an inappropriate or unhelpful response to major life stressors such as job loss, debt, abuse, separation, childbirth, relocation, etc.

However, not everyone gets depressed when faced with life stressors. This is because some of us are more predisposed to depression than others. Predispositions include our genes and physical make up, our upbringing, our culture, and whether we have instances of trauma or abuse in our past.

Social isolation is also associated with depression. When facing life's crises, having social support around you will make you more resilient to depression. On the other hand, going through major life stressors alone can make the strongest of us buckle. Remember that withdrawal is one of the symptoms of depression. So as depression takes hold, those affected move away from their networks of support.

Finally, there are issues around the behaviours we adopt when we are stressed. What do you do to unwind? Many of us turn to quick fixes like alcohol, caffeine, chocolate and nicotine to help us de-stress. This is fine in the short-term, but in time these will have a negative impact on health and add to depression.

Depression is most likely caused by a combination of predispositions, social isolation and quick fix behaviour, triggered by a major life stressor.

Impact of depression

As someone becomes depressed, they can find themselves caught up in a vicious circle in which the effects of the depression become a cause of further depression.

Depression impacts on people:

o   Socially

o   Physically

o   Emotionally

o   Cognitively.

The most common social effect is withdrawal. People with depression often isolate themselves from family and friends, and may neglect their responsibilities as employees, family members and neighbours. Isolation may also include not answering the telephone or the front door, and not opening letters and emails. Sometimes, people with depression will try to test the loyalty of people around them by saying or doing things that would drive them away. Of course, in time, this will have the opposite effect of that desired, and the person really will walk away!

The most troubling physical effects of depression are disrupted sleep and exhaustion. Depression can also result in digestive disorders, sexual dysfunction, muscle pains and headaches. In the longer term, depression is associated with a higher risk for a range of major illnesses including autoimmune diseases, cancer, diabetes, heart disease and strokes.

Emotional responses to depression can vary from psychic numbing to extreme sadness, guilt and hopelessness. These emotions can become overwhelming and can lead to thoughts of suicide.

Depression has a major effect on memory and concentration. It also results in a more negative outlook on life coupled to guilt and self-criticism. In more severe depression, people can experience persistent "negative automatic thoughts" which seriously trouble the person experiencing them.

Prognosis

Episodes of depression seldom last more than 2 years, and most people recover within 6 months. However, relapse is common. Half of those who have had an episode of depression will go on to have another. This rises to 75% for those who have had two episodes, and 95% for those who have had three or more episodes.

Self-management and appropriate treatment will promote recovery and prevent relapse.

Severe Mental Illness

Psychiatrists often use the term "severe mental illness" to describe psychotic illnesses. This mostly means two conditions:

o   Bipolar (or Manic) Depression

o   Schizophrenia.

These conditions are relatively rare, affecting around 3 percent of the population at some time in their lives.

Because these conditions are rare and misunderstood, those affected face particular problems with stigma and discrimination.

People with these conditions are often assumed to be dangerous. This is because terms (derived from Victorian diagnoses) like 'maniac' or 'psycho' are commonly used to describe violent criminals.

In the UK, violence and homicide remain rare. Indeed, the person most likely to attack or kill you is the person you share a bed with!

People with mental illness have a much greater risk of being a victim of homicide or serious assault than the general public.

Public perceptions of people with severe mental illness are also distorted because those with the most complex and enduring problems are also the most visible—those that the authorities refer to as 'revolving door patients' because they persistently fail to cope in the community following discharge from hospital. This leads to the false perception that people with mental illness are much more needy and dependent than is actually the case.

The majority of people with severe mental illness lead perfectly ordinary (and sometimes extraordinary) lives in the community. Although an exact number would be impossible to calculate, best estimates are that only a third of people with severe mental illness are receiving specialist mental health services at any time. A third do not need, and do not receive, any formal medical support. The remaining third are able to manage their condition using a combination of medication and self-management techniques.

There may also be a much larger group who have a single, short-lived experience of psychosis for which little (if any) medical support is sought or needed.

Initial diagnosis can be a problem with this group, as most psychotic illness is much more common in males than females, and first manifests between the ages of 15 and 25. As such, it can be mistaken for 'teenage angst' or even as evidence for illegal drug use. Also, because psychotic illness is episodic, many of the symptoms may only be present for relatively short periods. This can mean a gap of a year or more between symptoms first appearing and a medical professional making a diagnosis and providing essential treatment and support.

Since the prognosis for these conditions is much better when those affected receive early treatment, improved public awareness of them is essential.

Bipolar Depression

Bipolar Depression is a condition characterised by severe mood swings that can lift the mood of those affected to ecstatic highs, only to plunge them down into suicidal despair.

The downside to this is that someone experiencing an extreme high ('mania'), or even the upper edges of ordinary elation ('hypomania') is unlikely to seek or accept help.

Hypomania is a carefree state in which everything feels good, anything is possible, and nothing can go wrong. Those affected feel great, and can have a highly energising effect on people around them. However, hypomania can have a downside. Those affected may begin to engage in risky behaviours such as:

o   Excessive spending

o   Gambling

o   High risk business investments and practices

o   Casual sex.

For people that live with bipolar depression, this can be a warning sign that they are about to tip over into an episode of mania.

In mania, the 'high' gets out of control, and those affected can lose touch with reality. Symptoms include:

o   Increased energy

o   Decreased sleep

o   Irritability

o   Loss of inhibitions

o   Rapid thinking (causing the person to speak rapidly and incoherently)

o   Grandiose beliefs involving an inflated view of their abilities and place in/effect on the world around them

○ Lost contact with reality (coming to believe that their delusions and distorted beliefs are real, and refusing to accept they have a problem).

Manic episodes tend to be relatively short-lived—although during an episode, those affected can cause serious harm (economic, social and personal) to themselves and to their reputation.

Although people with bipolar depression can experience episodes of depression without a preceding manic episode, manic episodes are almost always followed be a descent into depression.

Because depression is more likely to be perceived as a problem for people with bipolar, it is much more likely that they will seek medical help at this point. This carries additional risks, as without knowledge of preceding mania a general practitioner may well diagnose (unipolar) depression. As a result, they may well prescribe an antidepressant that carries a risk of causing a new episode of mania.

Prognosis

Half of those who experience an episode of mania will recover within six months, and 98 percent will recover within two years. Unfortunately, about 40 percent go on to experience further episodes within two years of recovery, while 20 percent relapse immediately after recovery.

Early treatment is particularly effective in helping people recover from an episode. Also, a combination of (where necessary) mood stabilising drugs, antipsychotic drugs, psychological therapies and self-management can be very effective in preventing relapse. People who live with bipolar depression (and those around them) can learn how to spot and act on the warning signs before they get out of control. Bipolar UK offers a self-management training programme (see sources of support at the back of this book).

Schizophrenia

Although many still think people affected by schizophrenia have a 'split personality' (the term translates as 'fractured mind'), this is untrue, and misrepresents the experience of someone with the condition.

People with schizophrenia also suffer considerable stigma and discrimination because of media stereotypes that link the condition with violent behaviour. However, violent behaviour is not a feature of the condition.

Schizophrenia is characterised by episodes involving changes in emotions, thoughts and perceptions, and in changed behaviour. In some (but not all) cases, there may also be sensory distortions and hallucinations.

Symptoms of schizophrenia include:

- o Emotional changes such as:
- o 'Psychic numbing' - an inability to feel any emotion
- o Inappropriate emotions
- o Depression
- o Anxiety
- o Irritability
- o Suspicion (and sometime paranoia)
- o Changes in appetite
- o Reduced energy
- o Behaviour changes such as:
- o Withdrawal
- o Disturbed sleep
- o Inability to function in day to day life
- o Changes in thoughts and perception such as:

- ○ Loss of concentration and memory
- ○ Sensory distortion (for example seeing colours more vividly)
- ○ Mixed sensory experiences (for example seeing musical notes as colours)
- ○ Hallucinations (for example, hearing voices or seeing things that aren't real).
- ○ A sense that they, others, or the world around them have been altered.

As with bipolar depression, most people affected by schizophrenia live perfectly ordinary lives, some with the use of medication and support, others without the need for any formal support at all. It is only about a third of those affected who require in-patient or non-routine specialist support at any time.

In most cases, the symptoms of schizophrenia first manifest in mid to late teens. This can cause difficulties because the symptoms may be misinterpreted as teenage angst or as evidence of illegal drug use (which can also be a trigger for schizophrenia).

It is important that those affected by schizophrenia receive treatment and support as quickly as possible, as the prognosis is much better for those who receive early interventions, and those who can quickly be helped to self-manage the condition.

Mental Health Legislation

Unlike other illnesses, mental illness is covered by special legislation which allows the authorities to detain and treat someone with a mental illness against their will where they pose a risk to themselves or others.

Mass media have tended to link detention under the Mental Health Act to violent behaviour. But they are used most often to prevent someone (for example, a person with severe depression) from harming themselves or attempting suicide

In practice, this power is used sparingly, as the outcomes are much better for patients who cooperate with clinicians in developing and complying with a package of treatment and support.

Nevertheless, the existence of mental health legislation is a reminder that in a minority of instances, a person's mental illness may become so severe as to put their life or their health at risk.

Case Studies

In this section, we have looked at the various types of mental illness that you might encounter in the course of your family, social or work life. But faced with real life situations, would you be able to determine whether someone was displaying the warning signs or symptoms of mental illness?

The following case studies are designed to give you an insight into the kind of situation where you might be called upon to help. Read through them and see what you think. Try answering the questions at the end of each one.

Case Study 1

You have gone to visit a cousin whom you have not seen for a couple of months.

She used to be outgoing, and was quite active in her local community. But a couple of days ago, one of her neighbours told you that she seemed to be spending all of her time locked up in her house. Indeed, none of the neighbours can remember seeing her out and about for the last month or so – she has even taken to having her shopping delivered.

When you arrive, your cousin seems agitated, and insists you come in and quickly close the door behind you. Even though it is mid-afternoon, all of the curtains in the house are drawn.

Your cousin becomes very agitated when you suggest opening the curtains to let some light and fresh air into the room.

What might be happening to your cousin?

What are the risks if you do nothing?

Case Study 2

A friend confides to you that he is worried about his wife.

She has become quite withdrawn, even from her friends and family, and try as he might he cannot get her to take an interest in her usual pursuits. She gets irritated easily, but he is finding it difficult to get any other emotional response from her. He has suggested a family holiday "to cheer her up", but she says she doesn't want to travel.

She is often awake at night and spends the time downstairs alone. Last night he went down to sit with her, but she seemed so startled when he appeared in the room that he says he won't try this again.

Some months ago, she was first on the scene of a road accident in which a pedestrian was killed. But it wasn't anyone she knew, and the incident didn't affect her at the time, so he doesn't think this is significant.

What might be happening to your friend's wife?

What are the risks if you do nothing?

Case Study 3

You are going shopping with your teenage daughter.

You are queuing at the bus stop, when you notice that your daughter has become quite agitated. She is breathing rapidly, has sweat on her brow, and her face is flushed.

She says that something dreadful is going to happen, but cannot say what. She complains that she has a sharp pain on the left side of her chest, and thinks she is seriously ill.

What might be happening to your daughter?
What are the risks if you do nothing?

Case Study 4

You have been working alongside Jenny for some time, and you have always found her to be organised, hard-working, and cheerful by nature.

Recently she seems to have changed, though you can't pin down quite when this started. Her usual smile has gone, and she is looking tired and dishevelled. She is taking frequent coffee breaks. She seems unwilling to talk or even to make eye contact, and sometimes she looks as if she is close to tears.

Jenny lacks the enthusiasm she used to have for her work, and does not contribute to the team as she used to. She is missing deadlines, and is turning up at meetings clearly unprepared.

Last week you gave her some important information and a document to read in preparation for today's meeting, but she does not seem to know anything about this at all.

What might be happening to Jenny?

What are the risks if you do nothing?

Case Study 5

You phone a friend whom you have not seen for a while, and invite him out for a drink.

He seems reluctant but he sounds a bit down so you encourage him to come out as this might cheer him up. Over a pint he tells you that he was made redundant three months ago. He is clearly very upset about this, as he was dedicated to his work. He is looking for another job, but without much enthusiasm.

He says he feels as if he doesn't have a role in the world of work any more, and that his qualifications and years of experience have no value.

He says he feels lonely, even in his own home. He is missing his son, now in his first year at university. His daughter left home to live with her partner a year ago. His wife doesn't spend much time with him; she is always out, either at work, at the health club, or going out with her friends.

"If I were dead," he says," I doubt that anyone would notice?"

What might be happening to your friend?
What are the risks if you do nothing?

Case Study 6

A friend has confided to you that she is very concerned about her teenage son. He is spending a lot of time in his room and is avoiding the rest of the family, even at meal times, though he is heard moving about the house at night.

His friends are saying that they have not heard from him much either. He has missed weeks of football practice, and there has been no sight or sound of him playing his guitar.

Your friend says that her son did not do as well as expected in his recent exams, but apart from this she cannot see any reason for his current behaviour. She seems worried but at the same time frustrated by the situation. She says she hopes it's just a phase and that he'll soon "snap out of it."

What might be happening to your friend's son?

What are the risks if you do nothing?

In Case Study 1, your cousin is displaying several signs and symptoms of an anxiety disorder. Her situation suggests that she may be experiencing agoraphobia (a fear of open spaces).

Your cousin's agoraphobia may be a problem in and of itself, or it might be the result of depression or another anxiety disorder (the case study deliberately does not give sufficient detail to determine this).

Although most people with anxiety problems make a full recovery, getting early help is important. Unless your cousin recognises that she has a problem, and seeks appropriate help, it is unlikely that her problem will go away.

Because the agoraphobia is seriously interfering with your cousin's ability to engage with daily life, she faces considerable risks. In addition to the agoraphobia, she faces deteriorating health, loss of income, and the social consequences of prolonged withdrawal.

In Case Study 2, your friend's wife appears to have symptoms of both depression and anxiety. However, because she was at the scene of a road accident where someone was killed, this might indicate that she has Post Traumatic Stress Disorder (PTSD).

These days, treatment for PTSD is good, and the expectation is that your friend's wife will recover. However, this is unlikely to just happen. Left untreated, her condition may well deteriorate, and this can have a major impact on her ability to cope with life.

In Case Study 3, your daughter appears to be experiencing a panic attack. These are very common and are harmless, but can be very distressing for someone having one for the first time.

If this is a one-off panic attack, then there will be no further risk to your daughter. However, most people who experience panic attacks will have many attacks over an episode that can last months or even several years. If this were to happen, your daughter might develop a panic disorder that would seriously impact on her ability to get on with her life.

In Case Study 4, Jenny is displaying several of the symptoms and warning signs of depression. Although it is not clear (from the case study) whether something has caused Jenny to become depressed, it is clear that she is struggling to cope with the day-to-day demands of her job.

Almost everyone who experiences an episode of depression will recover within two years. However, the earlier they get appropriate help, the quicker recovery will be. It is important that Jenny recognise that she has a problem and begin to take steps to overcome her depression.

The risk to Jenny if nothing is done is quite serious. She is already under-performing in work. And although employment and disability legislation are meant to protect people like Jenny from being dismissed as a result of illness, many employers will initiate disciplinary procedures to deal with the drop in performance.

Were Jenny to lose her job, and be forced to live on a very low income, this is likely to have a seriously damaging effect on her health and well being.

In Case Study 5, your friend is displaying several of the symptoms and warning signs of depression. This seems to stem from his being made redundant three months ago.

He now seems to be very negative about his abilities and qualifications. He also seems to be withdrawn and disconnected from people he cares about.

There is a considerable risk that your friend's depression will continue to worsen, since he is isolated both socially and economically. This can only serve to make recovery more difficult.

You should be particularly concerned about his statement at the end of the case study: "If I were dead I doubt that anyone would notice?" This indicates that he may have been contemplating his own death, and may be a warning sign that he is considering suicide.

Suicide is a significant risk to people with mental illness, especially those who are depressed and those with severe mental illness. It is more prevalent in men than women, and is particularly associated with poverty.

With this in mind, it is essential that your friend seeks appropriate help as soon as possible.

Case Study 6 is (intentionally) a bit tricky. Your friend's son is certainly withdrawn, and this may be to do with his poor performance in his exams. This might indicate that he is depressed. However, many teenage boys behave strangely, feel alienated, and cause concern to their parents. Your friend may be right, this may be teenage angst and he may snap out of it.

On the other hand, there are considerable risks if this is depression. Your friend's son is at a crucial point in his education. Poor performance at this point may seriously damage his career prospects, and may leave him feeling even more depressed and alienated.

You should also remember that people who develop psychotic illnesses often have their first episode during their teens. While there is nothing definite in what your friend has said to indicate this, she may be leaving some important details out.

Since with both depression and psychotic illness recovery is easier where there is early treatment and appropriate support, you may want to encourage your friend to get her son to see a doctor.

The people in all of these case studies are displaying signs and symptoms of mental illnesses in ordinary settings. There is nothing clear cut about them. However, seeking or encouraging help cannot hurt, and it could be the difference between rapid recovery and a descent into despair.

How to Help

One of the biggest difficulties facing people with mental illness is that the people closest to them do not know what to do. Often, we do nothing because we are worried that we may say or do the wrong thing. But doing nothing is often the very worst thing we can do. Doing or saying nothing will confirm their low self-esteem, their belief that nobody cares about them, and their feeling that there is no point in asking for help.

Helping someone who is displaying the warning signs and symptoms of mental illness is important because:

o   Prevention and early intervention are more likely to result in long-term recovery.

o   Treatment can be slow, particularly where mental illness is severe

o   There are long waiting lists for specialist services

o   Those affected are at risk of losing:

o   Their employment

o   Their relationship

o   Their home.

So what can you do?

Here is a mnemonic to remember:

L.A.S.S.

Listen (without judging)
Assess (and if necessary, ask about suicide)

Signpost to appropriate sources of support

Self-help

Following these steps in turn will give you a model to use to help anyone who is experiencing mental distress.

Listen

You may remember the old British Telecom strap-line: "it's good to talk". For someone experiencing mental distress, this is especially so. Being able to give voice to what you are experiencing and—crucially—knowing that you are heard is an important step on the road to recovery.

So, listening to someone who is experiencing mental distress is the starting point for helping.

Listening is a skill that has to be learned. You may think that you listen to people when you are having a conversation. However, if you focus on what is happening to you during a conversation, you will find that you are not listening for a considerable part of the time when the other person is speaking. You will find that as they are speaking:

- o You are thinking about what you will say next
- o You are distracted by thoughts about things you were doing or things you have to do later
- o You become emotionally aroused in response to things they are saying (e.g., you might feel irritation, anger, concern, happiness, jealousy, etc)
- o Your body's physical sensations interrupt your chain of thought (e.g., you might notice an itch, or feel discomfort in your legs or arms)
- o Your mind drifts off onto other things.

Consciously focusing on what someone else is saying, without allowing these mental, emotional and physical processes to interfere is actually quite difficult.

It is helpful to consciously adopt a "listening mode" when you are helping someone who is experiencing mental distress. You might, for example:

- o Bring your attention to your body—focus on feeling your feet on the floor, then focus up through your body, on your legs, hips, back, tummy, chest, hands, arms, shoulders, neck, head, face and scalp
- o Make sure you are breathing deeply and slowly
- o Say to yourself, "I am focusing on listening now".

You should find that this helps you to focus on the here and now, and to be less distracted by the things that you had been doing or by thoughts about what you are going to do later.

Remember that the aim of this type of listening is to encourage the person you are with to open up, and to allow them to talk about their distress. As such, you do not want to respond to what they are saying as you would if you were having a conversation. Rather, you should encourage them to keep talking.

For example:

- o Respond in an open-ended manner. Use phrases like, "that sounds very painful" or "I can hear that you are in a great deal of distress"
- o Respond with questions such as, "That sounds very difficult, tell me more?" or "How does that make you feel?"
- o Use body language to show you are open, and want to know more. Gently nodding and moving your hand can also signal that you want them to keep talking.

Non-Judgemental Listening

It is important that you learn to suspend judgement when you are helping someone who is experiencing mental distress.

Remember that a key aspect of mental health problems is that they are not rational. As such, it is very likely that someone affected by mental illness will say things that you simply cannot understand or do not believe. What they say may even make you feel angry or upset. Nevertheless, what they are telling you is true for them.

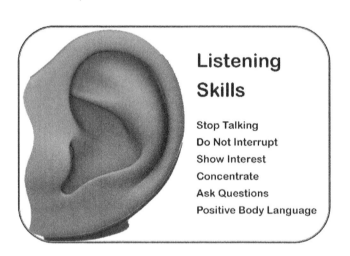

Listening Skills

Stop Talking
Do Not Interrupt
Show Interest
Concentrate
Ask Questions
Positive Body Language

Being non-judgemental means not responding to what someone is saying by:

- o Displaying your emotions through your body language
- o Answering back
- o Arguing
- o Contradicting
- o Allowing your posture to close.

This is easier said than done, as you need to be focused on consciously listening if you are to avoid giving away your thoughts and feelings through your body language or through a spontaneous quip before you have had time to check yourself.

This does not, of course, mean that you have to collude with what they are saying. Nor should you allow them to act on false beliefs if this might cause them harm.

Many people with mental illness will receive talking (psychological) therapies that will help them overcome unrealistic thoughts and beliefs. However, this is a skilled intervention that needs to be delivered carefully. Simply telling them they are wrong is not going to work, and will most likely result in their no longer wanting to talk about their problems with you.

Assess

Drawing on the information about mental illness in the first part of this book, you will be able to judge whether someone is displaying the warning signs or symptoms of a mental illness.

Remember that nobody expects you to act as a doctor or psychiatrist. Your role is similar to that of a first-aider in relation to physical health problems. In most instances, your role will be to provide a listening ear (and perhaps a shoulder to cry on) prior to encouraging them to seek appropriate support and to engage in the many self-help techniques that have been shown to help people recover from mental illness.

What you do need to assess is:

o   The impact their problem is having on their ability to get on with their life

o   What support they have available to them

o   Whether there is a risk of suicide.

Stigma and mental illness

In an ideal world, people with mental illness would be able to talk about their problems openly. In our world, if they do so, they face discrimination, isolation and in many cases violence and abuse.

While there are many brave individuals who have "come out" about their mental illness, this is not something that we can force upon others. Nor should we take lightly the additional problems that someone can face when they are given the label "mentally ill". (Remember that this label stays on people's records long after they have recovered).

Stigma is a key reason for assessing the impact that someone's problem is having on their ability to get on with their life. Clearly, if (because of a mental illness) someone is unable to hold down a job, their relationship is breaking down and their housing is at risk, then they need all the help that they can get—we can worry about stigma later on. If, at the other end of the spectrum, they are able to get on with their lives, then it is entirely up to them how they wish to address their problem—including whether they wish to seek formal medical support.

Remember that 80 percent of people with common mental illnesses and 30 percent of people with severe mental illnesses are able to recover without formal medical support (although they cannot know if they are in this group in advance).

So while we should not let fear of stigma and discrimination stand in the way of getting appropriate support when it is needed, we have to allow those with mental illness to make informed choices about seeking support.

Sources of support

There is a range of potential help available to someone experiencing mental distress. The most important sources are those that are "naturally occurring". These might include close friends, family, neighbours, work colleagues, and acquaintances known through leisure activities.

Provided that these potential supporters have the necessary information and skills, they can do a great deal to help someone they care about recover from mental illness. They can do this in two important ways:

o Encouraging them to engage with treatment
o Encouraging them to engage in self-help.

Because people in the "naturally occurring help" group are closer, and have more day-to-day contact, they are much better placed to give ongoing support during their recovery.

Other forms of support are more formal, and include:

o Charities and voluntary groups
o Employment support agencies
o General Practice
o Specialist Community Mental Health Teams (CMHTs)
o Private mental health services.

The support available will vary depending on where you live. For example, many charities run patient-led self-management groups. Others run voluntary counselling services. However, because these services are run by volunteers, they are not available throughout the country. Moreover, some services can have long waiting lists, particularly in areas where formal NHS services are in short supply.

General Practice is usually the first point of contact with the NHS. Initial assessment will either be by a doctor or (in some parts of the country) a "gateway worker". If a mental illness is diagnosed, they may be able to offer treatment and support within the practice. This might include:

- o Medication
- o Counselling
- o Computerised talking therapies
- o Books on prescription
- o Exercise on prescription
- o Expert Patient Programme training.

In most cases, mental illness is treated entirely within general practice. However, where a condition is severe or treatment resistant, or where there may be a risk of suicide, the doctor will make a referral to a specialist CMHT.

The CMHT is made up of people from across several specialisms including psychiatry, psychology, mental health nursing, occupational therapy, physiotherapy and social work. The CMHT can offer a targeted package of care using treatments and support that are not available in general practice.

NHS services are in short supply in many areas of the UK. This means that even when someone's need is recognised, they may not be able to secure appropriate treatment and support for several months. For this reason, it is worth considering what alternative provision might be available.

In some areas, employment agencies like Job Centre Plus can provide access to Cognitive Behavioural Therapy more readily than general practice. So where someone is currently unemployed or incapacitated and their mental illness is a factor, this avenue is worth exploring.

Where someone is in employment, their employer may offer psychological support either directly or through an "Employee Assistance Programme". Again, access to support through an employer will be much quicker than through the NHS.

If they are a member of a scheme like BUPA, or if they have a medical insurance policy, they may find that they are entitled to private psychological support. If not, they may also want to think about paying for private support if they have the means to do so. Unlike the NHS, there is no waiting list for private mental health services.

Ask About Suicide

Although suicide is rare, it is second only to accidents as a non-natural killer. More people in the UK (5,000) kill themselves every year than die in road traffic accidents (3,000).

Mental illness is the factor most closely linked to suicide. So, when someone with a mental illness says something along the lines of "you'd be better off without me", it is important to treat this seriously.

But how can you be sure whether they mean that they want to kill themselves or if they are just speaking figuratively?

There is only one way—*you must ask them*.

But asking about suicide is something of a taboo, even among people who work with those affected by mental illness. Nevertheless, asking directly is the only way of telling if they intend killing themselves.

Remember:

> **You cannot make someone suicidal just by asking.**
> **You might save someone's life by letting them know that you want to help them, and that you will not be shocked that they are thinking about ending their life.**

It is important to be direct—"are you going to kill yourself" is preferable to "are you thinking about..." Using the term "kill yourself" is much better than the more clinical/judicial term "commit suicide".

Asking about suicide is much easier if you are confident about how you will respond if they say yes! Another mnemonic that is useful here is:

P.I.M.S.

Plan

Immediacy

Means

Support

Do they have a **plan**? While not having a plan at the moment does not mean there is no threat, having a plan means the threat is much more urgent. It means they have thought this through, and may have decided to go ahead with this course of action.

If they have a plan, is the threat **immediate**? This will determine how much time you have to mobilise support.

Do they have the **means** to kill themselves? Killing yourself is actually much harder than you might suppose. In the last couple of decades, there has been a concerted effort to minimise access to means of killing yourself. For example, you can only buy drugs like Paracetamol in small quantities. Many public buildings have removed ligature points (to prevent hanging) and restricted access to roof space (to prevent jumping).

While it is hard to kill yourself, it can never be entirely prevented. Also, some people have better access to the means than others. For example, the three professions with the highest rates of suicide are doctors, vets and farmers. This is because each has ready access to poisons (and guns in the case of farmers) in the course of their day-to-day work.

Immediacy and access to means will determine the type of **support** you might be able to mobilise.

Clearly, in the unlikely event of your having to help someone who is stood on the edge of a high building threatening to jump, your options are limited. If you are alone, the best you can do is encourage them to talk and (if you have the opportunity) call the emergency services (999) for help (if someone else is with you, get them to do this).

In this type of circumstance, it is important:

o   Not to leave them on their own
o   Not to get physically involved
o   To get professional help as soon as possible.

Remember that others may be better qualified than you (but don't make this an excuse not to act). If there are other people around, ask if anyone has a background in mental health or the emergency services. There might also be someone who has completed the Applied Suicide Intervention Skills Training (ASIST) course provided by Living Works.

Where the risk is less immediate, you may be able to mobilise a wider network of support. For example, they may already be receiving services for mental illness through general practice or a CMHT. If so, you will be able to get them an emergency appointment with someone who is already supporting them. If they are not already receiving services, you can get an emergency appointment with the GP or you can access the duty psychiatrist via the local Accident and Emergency department.

Alcohol, drugs and suicide

Alcohol or drug use by someone at risk of suicide is a particular problem because these substances can seriously cloud their judgment (making a decision to kill themselves seem appropriate) while lowering their natural fear of death (making them more likely to act).

Remove the alcohol or drugs and you lower the risk of suicide. So where possible, you should encourage them to stop drinking or using drugs (both in the short and longer term).

Suicide "do's and don'ts" checklist

Do:

- ✓ Ask about suicide (PIMS)
- ✓ Try to reduce the risk
- ✓ Encourage them to talk
- ✓ Show that you are prepared to listen without judging
- ✓ Tell them you care and are willing to help
- ✓ Focus on getting them through the immediate crisis rather than worrying about the long-term
- ✓ Agree to reasonable requests
- ✓ Ask if there is someone they would particularly like to speak to (e.g., a friend, family member, medical practitioner or support worker).

Don't:

- ✗ Express shock
- ✗ Judge, criticise or blame
- ✗ Dare them to do it
- ✗ Talk about the sanctity of life
- ✗ Use guilt to try to dissuade them

    ✖   Leave them until you are sure the crisis has passed or
        appropriate support has arrived

    ✖   Be bound to secrecy.

This final point can be difficult, as we are usually taught to respect people's privacy and to keep secret things we are told in confidence. However, it is important to speak out where someone has threatened to kill themselves. Even if the immediate crisis has passed, the underlying mental illness and the socio-economic problems underlying this are still in place. Unless these are dealt with, the person may well become suicidal again in the near future.

Ideally, you should encourage the person to seek help for themselves—the prognosis for mental illness is much better where those affected are fully engaged with their treatment. However, where the person refuses to seek help, the medical authorities have powers under the Mental Health Act to take them to a place of safety until the risk of suicide has gone.

Mental Illness and Self-Harm

Self-harm is often thought of as being related to suicide. In fact, the two are poles apart. Whereas suicide is about ending life, self-harm is most often a (inappropriate) way of feeling alive and in control.

When we think about self-harming behaviour, we are most likely to think about severe forms such as:

- Cutting
- Burning
- Biting
- Hair pulling.

However, these are the severe end of a continuum that at one time or another almost all of us have been on. Think for a moment about times in your life when you have been particularly stressed or distressed, and ask yourself did you ever:

o Over-eat (particularly junk or comfort food)?

o Smoke?

o Drink too much?

o Over-work?

o Bite your nails?

o Play very loud music?

All of these are harmful (though less immediate than those above) ways of relieving stress.

Other methods include driving too fast or engaging in dangerous sports. These give you an immediate sense of relief (assuming you survive). Someone who is self-harming is seeking a similar sense of relief and aliveness using a method that they have learned and which may be the only means available to them.

Helping someone who is self-harming

Many people who self-harm are very secretive about what they are doing. As such, if they have decided that they trust you enough to disclose this to you, it is essential that you listen non-judgementally.

Do not dismiss self-harm as "attention seeking" or threaten not to help unless they stop doing it.

People who self-harm are likely to need specialist help to recover from their problems. However, you can help them by providing a listening ear and by encouraging them to stick with their programme of treatment and support.

Helping Someone who is Having a Panic Attack

Panic attacks are very common (affecting about 50 percent of us at some time in our lives) and are harmless (but extremely disturbing for those who experience them). A panic attack is an extreme manifestation of the body's fight or flight response.

The main symptoms of a panic attack are:

o   Increased heart rate (often with palpitations)

o   Rapid, shallow breathing

o   Sweating, trembling and shaking

o   Choking and a feeling of being unable to breathe

o   Chest pain or discomfort

o   Nausea

o   Feeling dizzy, light headed or faint

o   Feeling of detachment or unreality

o   Fear of death.

Although these symptoms may be triggered by cues in the environment, they are out of proportion to the actual threat involved. For example, two of the most common situations in which people have panic attacks are in crowded supermarkets or public transport. Although these can be trying and stressful, they do not warrant panic.

The immediate issues when helping someone who is experiencing a panic attack are:

o   Establishing that they are not having a heart attack or an asthma attack

o   Helping them to calm down.

Where the person is not known to you, or your relationship is not particularly intimate, you will want to err on the side of caution and either dial 999 or take them to A&E so that they can rule out any underlying physical health problem.

Where you have a closer relationship with the person, you might want to ask whether anything like this has happened before. It may well be that they have experienced panic attacks in the past. They will also be able to tell you if they have heart problems or asthma.

Although you will want them to get their heart checked out if you and they are unsure what is happening, there are some obvious differences between the symptoms of a heart attack and a panic attack. The most obvious is the difference in skin colour—in a heart attack oxygenated blood cannot get to the extremities, causing the skin to take on an ashen grey-blue-green tone. In a panic attack, the reverse is happening—too much oxygenated blood is being pumped to the extremities, causing the skin to take on a mottled pink and white tone (this is particularly obvious when looking at their palms).

In order to help someone who is having a panic attack to calm down:

o   Make eye contact and speak calmly and clearly
o   If possible, move them to quieter more private surroundings (or at least ask other people to move back)
o   Encourage them to sit down
o   Breathe slowly and deeply, and encourage them to breathe with you
o   Explain what a panic attack is, that it is common, and that it is not harmful.

It is rare for a panic attack to last longer than 15 minutes simply because the human body cannot continue to operate a fight or flight response for much longer. However, a panic attack may be an indication of an underlying anxiety problem. There is also a risk that the affected person may seek to avoid further panic attacks by withdrawing from situations that they think may trigger them. For these reasons, it is important to encourage them to seek appropriate support and to engage in self-help.

Seeking Appropriate Support

A panic attack most clearly demonstrates how mental illness (anxiety) and physical illness (asthma or a heart attack) might be confused. However, the symptoms of most forms of mental illness can also be symptoms of underlying physical health problems such as diabetes, liver disease, and thyroid problems.

This is one of the reasons why encouraging them to see their GP at an early stage is important. Their GP will want to rule out these potentially serious physical conditions before starting treatment for a mental illness.

Moreover, the earlier you intervene with a mental illness, the less severe it is likely to become and the more rapidly recovery will take place.

For most of us, the GP is the point of access for a range of mental health treatments and services such as:

○ Medication
○ Counselling
○ Cognitive Behavioural Therapy
○ Exercise on prescription
○ Books on prescription.

It is also the GP who will decide whether to refer to the CHMT for more intense specialist mental health services.

In addition to making referrals to health specialists, a good GP will also signpost to other sources of support outside the NHS. These might include:

○ Mental health charities

o   Mental health projects

o   Self-help groups

o   General health-related groups (e.g., green gyms, Weight Watchers, exercise classes).

The GP may also be able to give information about local private providers.

Mental health charities are a particularly useful resource, as they tend to approach mental illness from the patient's perspective. As such, they may be much more aware of what services are available locally, and may be better able to recommend these than are GPs.

I have given a list of national mental health charities at the end of this book (each will be able to give you details of branches or groups in your locality).

Self-Help

Self-help is the final element of our **LASS** mnemonic. For many people it is the most important. This is because most mental illness is self-healing. That is, given time, and assuming the stressors that triggered the episode have been removed, most people recover.

Seen in this way, the main issue in dealing with mental illness is to understand:

What promotes recovery?
What stands in the way of recovery?

At this point, you might expect me to reel off a list of each. Unfortunately, things are not so simple. What works for one person may not work for another—or may even stand in the way of recovery.

Consider the most famous of treatments for mental illness—Prozac. It is more than 25 years since the UK approved this antidepressant and by a host of "me-too" antidepressants followed. However, controversy continues to surround this family of drugs. On the one side are researchers, medical practitioners and patients who have benefited hugely from using these drugs. On the other are researchers, medical practitioners and patients who have seen appalling side effects and withdrawal symptoms with little apparent benefit to the underlying mental illness.

It is impossible to know which group you will be in before you take one of these drugs. However, the odds are that you will benefit (otherwise they would not have been approved by NICE), but nobody can guarantee that you will not be in the minority for whom they make things worse.

The only way you can know for sure is to try them.

The same is true for everything else that has been shown to help people recover from mental illness.

For example, engaging in physical activity can promote recovery. But it doesn't work for everyone, and it can be harmful to some people. The same can be said of diet, gardening, talking therapies, arts and crafts, working in green space and attending self-help groups.

In the end, it is only the person affected by mental illness who will be able to decide whether what they are doing is promoting recovery or whether it is standing in their way. The important thing is to give it a try.

When encouraging someone to engage in self-help, it is worth revisiting the model of the "personal burden" set out at the beginning of this book:

- o **Social Engagement**
- o **Physical Health**
- o **Emotional Health**

- o **Thoughts and Beliefs**
- o **Core Skills and Abilities**

It is important that they engage in activities that promote wellbeing in each area of their being.

Reverse social withdrawal

A key warning sign/symptom of mental illness is disengagement and withdrawal from social and economic life. However, withdrawal is always a downward spiral—the more they disengage, the harder it becomes to re-engage.

In work, for example, disengagement may begin with "presenteeism" (the process of being in work, but not working). It may also involve not socialising at work and withdrawing from team activities. Eventually, this may develop into absenteeism as they find excuses not to be at work—claiming a cold or an upset stomach perhaps. Because of the sickness monitoring used by many employers, there is a limit to how long someone can get away with this form of absenteeism. In the end, they may need to visit their GP to get a sick note if they are to continue being absent. This may lead to full-time absenteeism and may ultimately lead them to lose their job to long-term sickness.

A similar process of gradual disengagement and withdrawal will occur in other social circumstances such as withdrawal from family, friends, recreation, and even from intimate relationships.

Left for too long, they may well become housebound or nearly housebound—something that is considerably easier in an age of high speed broadband, supermarket home delivery and benefits paid by bank transfer.

Self-help in this area means re-engaging even if it feels difficult or emotionally painful.

In work, this might mean taking advantage of the "fit note" regime that began in 2010, through which a GP can declare someone to be sick, but able to engage in limited work. This might allow someone to re-engage on different hours or in a different role until they are ready to return to their previous work.

Social engagement outside work can be resumed similarly, starting with limited participation in order to build resilience and eventually being able to socialise fully again.

It is useful, for example, to set time limits on social activities. For example, they may agree to meet a friend for a coffee or glass of wine, but not want to agree to spend a whole evening out.

In recreation, it is important that they re-engage with activities that they know they used to enjoy even if their mental illness is preventing them from feeling enjoyment just at the moment. They should also be open to new experiences, even if their mental illness makes them think that they will not enjoy them.

When encouraging someone to help themselves, it is helpful to remind them that their social withdrawal is most likely a result of their mental illness rather than any objective problem with the person or situation they are re-engaging with.

Get physical

The separation of "mental" and "physical" illness can often mislead. The most troubling symptoms of mental illness are often the physical ones:

o   Disrupted sleep

o   Exhaustion

o   Digestive problems

o   Headaches

o   General aches and pains.

There is a great deal that can be done to address physical wellbeing, and this, in turn, can promote recovery from mental illness.

Most medical treatments are physical in nature. For example, many medications work by rebalancing chemicals in the brain and nervous system. Less common treatments such as Electro-Convulsive Therapy (ECT), Transcranial Magnetic Stimulation (TMS) and Vagus Nerve Stimulation (VNS) change the way the brain and nervous system operate.

From a self-help point of view, these medical treatments should be viewed in the same way as everything else:

Do they promote or maintain positive mental health? Or,

Do they make mental illness worse?

If the person you are helping is not benefiting from a particular treatment, encourage them to discuss this with their medical practitioner. There may be alternatives available, and it would be unethical to continue using a treatment if it is making things worse.

Exercise

There are many physical things that any one of us can do and that are known to have a positive effect on mental health for most people. The most simple of these is ensuring we get enough daylight and fresh air every day.

Simple things like sitting in the garden, walking to the shops or going to a local park can help lift mood, and are unlikely to do any harm.

Moving the body and using muscles are also important to maintaining and improving wellbeing. This does not necessarily have to involve formal exercise. Nor does it have to be costly or time consuming. Simple day to day tasks count as physical activity. For example:

- o Pushing the vacuum cleaner
- o Mopping the floor
- o Digging the garden
- o Cleaning the windows
- o Washing the car.

Going for a walk is another easy and cost-effective way of being physically active.

Other reasonably cost-effective forms of exercise include:

- o Swimming
- o Cycling
- o Jogging.

If cost is an issue, it is worth checking what classes and facilities are available from your local leisure centre. Leisure centres are often subsidised in order to keep them accessible to people on lower incomes. They may also operate discount or free access schemes for people on benefits and pensions.

In some parts of the UK, the NHS and local authorities have developed "Exercise on Prescription" schemes for people with mental health problems. These schemes are free, and involve regular sessions with a fitness instructor over a 6-8 week period during which a personal fitness regime is developed.

Ideally we should all engage in three types of physical activity or exercise every week:

- o Aerobic exercise (which involves moving the body in ways that increases the heart and breathing rate) such as walking, running and cycling.
- o Contraction exercises (that work and strengthen muscles) such as weight lifting and circuit training

o   Stretching exercises (that help maintain flexibility and promote relaxation) such as tai chi and yoga.

In practice, it would be difficult to find the time to do formal classes in all of these activities every week. Moreover, trying to do too much too quickly can make mental illness worse. This is an important reason for thinking carefully before joining a gym or fitness club. Most gyms and fitness clubs depend on people paying a monthly fee on a 12 or 18 month contract, but not actually using the facilities (these people effectively subsidise the minority of members who have the time and inclination to use the facilities every day).

It is common for someone with a mental illness to engage in a kind of "all or nothing" approach to their lives which results in their signing up with things believing they will commit fully to them, only to find that they cannot maintain so high a level of commitment, and then dropping out altogether.

If you are encouraging someone to be more physically active, it is important that they build their activity gradually. Rather than paying money to join a club or purchase sports equipment, they are better off starting with regular walking, jogging or swimming at their own pace while they recover a good degree of fitness.

It is also essential that being physically active is enjoyable. There is no point encouraging someone to do something that they didn't like doing before they became ill. On the other hand, if there were activities they used to enjoy, it is important to encourage them to re-engage with these.

Posture

Posture—the way we hold our bodies—is affected by the fight or flight mechanism that is involved in stress. Because people affected by mental illness tend to live with stress, their posture can settle into a stress-related crouch (see the image below).

In a stressful situation, the muscles will tense (preparing the body to spring into action) the fists will tighten, as will the muscles in the arms, shoulders, neck, back and legs.

In a stressful situation, the body will also adopt a defensive crouch. The front of the body will curl over, protecting the vital organs, and leaving the back (where less damage can be done) more open.

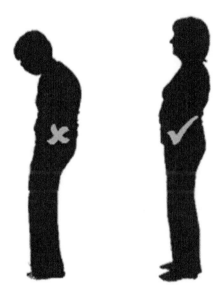

If someone remains stressed often enough and for long enough they will begin to adopt a posture similar to the one on the left of the picture. The picture on the right shows a correct, open posture.

Posture quite literally affects your outlook on life. You can try this for yourself. Adopt a stressed crouch like that on the left. Your shoulders hunched over and your head dropped down. Without changing the posture, check your field of vision. Then open out into a posture like that on the right, and see how much more you can see.

In addition, a stressed crouch has a negative impact on wellbeing by constricting vital organs, making them less efficient and forcing them to work harder.

Encouraging someone to regularly stretch into an open posture is easily overlooked, but it is a simple thing that can make a big difference to their sense of wellbeing.

If they have a particular problem with posture, you might want to encourage them to try Alexander technique, Pilates, tai chi or yoga, which all help to re-align posture.

Breathing

Stress and mental illness often result in poor breathing. We are seldom aware of how and where we are breathing because breath is an almost automatic process. We do not have to remember to breathe, it just happens.

Stress results in rapid, shallow breathing in the upper part of the lung, at the top of the chest. This is similar to the panting breath that you experience when you are exercising.

The body uses this type of breath to quickly circulate oxygen to the muscles. So this type of breathing also requires increased heart rate and dilation of the arteries.

This is fine if you are exercising or if you have to escape danger. But when (as a result of an on-going stress response) the body settles into this type of breathing as the norm, it can damage health and wellbeing. Extra strain is put on the heart, and toxic carbon dioxide is not being fully expelled from the lung. Over time, lung capacity is also impaired.

Fortunately, because we can consciously over-ride the way our bodies breathe, it is possible to re-learn a calmer and healthier way of breathing.

This is an area where a good yoga class will be of help, as breathing exercises are a core element of yoga, and these have been shown to be of benefit to people affected by mental illness. However, there are some simple breathing techniques that you can learn and encourage others to try:

Start by sitting upright but comfortably in a chair. Try to hold your head up with your eyes looking straight ahead. Place one hand on your belly (over or just below your navel). Place the other hand at the centre of your chest so the palm is touching your sternum (breast bone). Close your eyes or lower your gaze. Then bring your attention to the sensation of the breath at your nose. Next, notice the sensation of the breath as it comes in through the nose, throat and down into the lungs. Then watch as the breath leaves the lungs, throat and nose. Once you are used to this, imaging that as the breath comes in, it is pulled down to your hands—feel the belly gently rise and move your hand forward, then feel your chest move your other hand gently forward and slightly upward. Do not force the breath. Just allow the breath to gently ebb and flow, moving your hands with each breath.

This technique will encourage the use of the whole of the lung. It will also slow the breathing, lower the heart rate, and help you relax. It can be particularly useful for someone experiencing a panic attack.

Relaxation

All too often, we think that we are relaxing when we sit in front of the TV or a computer. Indeed, many of us regard anything that we do that is not work-related as "relaxation". But genuine relaxation involves allowing the body to let go of stress and tension and getting the mind to quieten and become calm. This is much more difficult to achieve. And it is particularly difficult for someone who is experiencing mental distress.

It is important to learn to relax naturally, rather than using alcohol or drugs (prescription or illegal). While these offer a short-term fix, they lead to poor mental and physical health in the longer term. Alcohol is a depressant drug—prolonged use will trigger depression and anxiety. Illegal drugs have been linked to mental illness, and are a really bad idea for someone who is already experiencing mental distress.

The starting point for learning to relax is to set a regular time aside. This need only be 10-20 minutes. However, it is important that this time is protected so that relaxation will not be interrupted.

It is also helpful to find a comfortable space to use for relaxation. Ideally, this should be uncluttered, not too warm or cold and well ventilated.

Each of us has to find out for ourselves whether we prefer to sit or lie down, and whether we are going to use the floor or whether we will use a chair or bed. All that matters is to find what is most comfortable and stick to it.

Some people are able to relax without any additional aid, just by tensing and un-tensing their muscles, and letting their mind empty. Others will use a relaxation CD (this might involve a spoken relaxation or it might just be relaxing sounds and music). Bio-feedback relaxation machines can be particularly effective relaxation aids, but they can also be very expensive.

Many people turn to complementary therapies such as aromatherapy, massage and reflexology to help them relax. Others participate in gentle exercise such as tai chi and yoga, which also promote relaxation.

Most people find trying to relax particularly difficult to begin with. Usually, the body will not let go of its tension and the mind will not quieten down. This is why sticking to a routine is important.

Gradually, body and mind get into the habit of letting go. So when encouraging someone to relax, you must also encourage them to stick with it.

Sleep

Nobody is altogether sure what sleep is for. However, it seems likely that sleep fulfils three different functions:

- In children and adolescents, periods of deep sleep allow the developing body to grow
- Deep sleep also allows the body to repair itself
- Periods of Rapid Eye Movement (REM) sleep seem to be tied up with mental health, allowing emotions to be processed and memories to be stored.

In the course of an ordinary night's sleep, we all go through several periods of deep sleep and REM sleep.

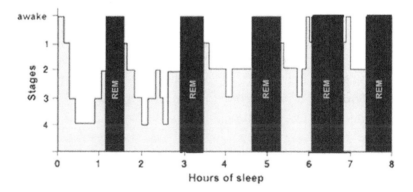

Many people affected by mental distress are different. They often struggle to get off to sleep, experience waking in the early hours, and are exhausted during the day. It is believed that this is because their distress causes them to need more REM sleep to allow additional emotional processing. This means their sleep is restless and disrupted. It also means that they are not getting sufficient rejuvenating deep sleep.

Because REM sleep uses more energy than being awake, their system eventually wakes them up (usually in the early hours). The experience of this is of being mentally alert but physically exhausted.

Understandably, people who experience this night after night will often try to "catch up" on lost sleep during the following day. Unfortunately, this sets up further problems by making it harder to sleep the following night.

People who experience this type of disrupted sleep will often turn to caffeine (or other stimulant drugs) to help them stay awake during the day, and to alcohol, sleeping pills or tranquilisers to help them sleep at night. Unfortunately, these have a negative impact on health, and result in an artificial sleep that is neither refreshing nor rejuvenating.

Where sleep is a particular problem, a doctor can prescribe a sleeping tablet, a tranquiliser or an antidepressant (such as Mirtazapine) that causes drowsiness in order to address the immediate problem. However, these days doctors are advised against long-term use because of the risk of addiction and because of the risks to long-term health.

More often, doctors will encourage better "sleep hygiene" (essentially learning a healthy sleep routine):

o   Go to bed at the same time every night
o   Keep the bedroom uncluttered, well ventilated, fragrant and not too hot or cold
o   Only use the bedroom for sleep
o   Make sure it is quiet and dark enough for sleep
o   Don't have a TV or computer in the bedroom
o   Don't have a clock in the room (if you need an alarm clock, put it out of reach and out of sight).

It is important to prepare for sleep rather than just going to bed and expecting sleep to happen. Each of us has to learn how to prepare for ourselves, as what works for you may not work for me.

Some suggestions include:

o   Have a warm milky drink and a biscuit before bed

o   Have a warm bath

o   Do some exercise earlier in the evening (but avoid anything strenuous immediately before bed)

o   Read for 30-60 minutes before lights out.

It is best to avoid caffeine after 6.00pm so that the stimulant effect will have worn off before bed time. It is also best to avoid a heavy meal late in the evening.

Some people find the scent of aromatherapy oils such as lavender or ylang ylang to help promote sleep (although this is often a matter of individual taste). Others find herbal teas and preparations such as Kalms helpful in getting off to sleep.

Learning to address worries can also help. One approach to this that many people use is to keep a pen and paper next to the bed to write down any worries that get in the way of sleep. These must then be dealt with in the morning—often people find that problems that appeared enormous in the dead of night turn out to be easily dealt with when looked at in daylight.

Getting into a sleep routine can be difficult to begin with. It may take several weeks before any change occurs. Even then, it may be just a couple of good nights dotted between the usual run of bad ones. But with time, the number of good nights will overtake the number of bad ones.

If you are helping someone to adopt a healthier sleep routine, it is important to encourage them to stick with it.

Be creative with emotions

One of the difficulties with viewing stress, anxiety and depression as illness is that we tend to forget that they are often an entirely normal human response to difficult life events.

There comes a point where all of us (faced with enough stress for long enough) need to withdraw in order to lick our wounds and repair our lives. Unfortunately, a by-product of this withdrawal is to turn feelings in upon you.

The mental distress that we are trying to help with can often be as much to do with the turning in of emotions like anger, sadness, desolation and hate, as to external stressors. This is why two people can go through almost identical circumstances with totally different outcomes.

For example, two people made redundant from the same firm may experience redundancy very differently. One sees redundancy as a mark of personal failure—"if only I'd worked harder or done more to impress management, they would have kept me on". The other sees it as just one of the vagaries of global capitalism—"there is nothing personal about it, the people who made the decision knew nothing about me".

The first person may well descend in to a vicious circle of self-blame, self-doubt and self-hatred that, in turn, will lead to a depression that stands in the way of finding alternative employment. This will serve to reinforce their original negative emotions.

Unfortunately, many of us are not truly in touch with our emotions. We go into a state of disassociation or denial when we experience things that make us angry, frustrated or hurt. A healthier approach is to be aware of emotions in order to work through them.

For someone experiencing mental distress, the simplest thing to do is to talk. By listening to them, we can help them get in touch with what they are feeling, and to give voice to their emotions.

For some people, talking may be enough. For others, it can be helpful to encourage them to engage in other healthy means of expressing their emotions. These might include creative activities such as:

- Keeping a diary
- Writing poetry
- Art and crafts
- Playing or writing music
- Photography.

Activities like these provide a healthy and socially acceptable means of giving voice to feelings as an alternative to turning them in upon oneself or (worse still) becoming angry, or hurtful to other people.

Deal with unhelpful thoughts and beliefs

It is important to remember that one of the defining characteristics of mental health problems is that they are irrational. Unrealistic and often negative thoughts and beliefs are common to people affected by all types of mental illness.

In the case of severe mental illness, thoughts and beliefs may be very obviously distorted. For example, someone affected by schizophrenia during an episode of the illness may believe that the government is tracking him via the television, or may believe that people around her have changed or been changed in some way. Someone experiencing mania during an episode of bipolar depression may believe with absolute certainty that a particular horse is going to win the Grand National, and may see nothing wrong with gambling his life savings on it.

Although not always present, paranoia is a common mental state for many people affected by mental illness. Where someone is experiencing paranoia, they can be particularly difficult to help, as they may well distrust your motives and may be fearful of health and social care professionals.

Clearly, there would be adverse consequences if people who experience such delusional thoughts and beliefs were to act upon them. As such, while acknowledging that you understand the person thinks or believes these things, you should never collude with them.

Thoughts associated with common mental illnesses may seem less delusional, but can also be very disabling. Indeed, distorted (often negative) thoughts that seem to have some apparent basis in reality are more credible both to those affected and to people around them.

You can help someone who is experiencing negative and unrealistic thoughts by helping them to look at their thoughts more objectively. To do this, it is helpful to be aware of the different ways in which thoughts become distorted.

There are 10 broad forms of distorted thoughts:

1. All or nothing thoughts
2. Labelling
3. Over-generalisation
4. Mental filtering
5. Discounting the positive
6. Jumping to conclusions
7. Magnification
8. Emotional reasoning
9. Should/must/ought thoughts
10. Personalisation and blame.

All or nothing thoughts

With all or nothing thinking there is no such thing as second best. Either something is perfect or lives up to an ideal, or it is rubbish.

Someone who thinks in this way is bound to be disappointed because life seldom lives up to our ideals. We do not have perfect jobs, relationships, homes, neighbourhoods, holidays, etc. Most of us settle for situations in which the positives far outweigh the negatives. We see that just because something is not ideal does not mean that it is bad.

Labelling

Labelling involves internalising the negative, and is related to all or nothing thinking. Someone who believes things haven't turned out well will give themselves labels such as, "I am a fool" or "I am incompetent".

Even if someone has done something foolish, that does not make them a "fool" (with the implication that they will always do foolish things). Usually, they did what they did with the best intentions, and were trying their best. Often, things did not turn out as bad as they believe.

Over-generalisation

Over-generalisation involves taking a single incident and projecting it onto the whole of your life. For example, if you attend a job interview but are ultimately rejected, you come to think "I am unemployable". Similarly, you ask someone out on a date and they turn you down so you think "I am unlovable".

In reality, it might just be that the person you asked out on a date did not fancy you, or had other reasons (perhaps they were already seeing someone) for not accepting. Similarly, you may have had the misfortune to be competing for a job with someone who had slightly better qualifications or a bit more experience than you.

Mental filtering

Mental filtering means giving greater weight to some kinds of information than to others. For example, if you believe you are "unlovable", "unemployable", "a fool" or "incompetent", then you look for evidence that this is so while dismissing any evidence that would suggest that it is not.

Discounting the positive

Discounting the positive is related to mental filtering, and involves totally rejecting evidence that disproves a negative belief about yourself or your life. For example, having decided that you are "unemployable", you might dismiss the knowledge, skills and experience that you have built up during your life. This may well lead to your not applying for jobs that you might be suited to, which would tend to confirm your belief that you are unemployable.

Jumping to conclusions

This means forming a belief about something on the basis of incomplete information. For example, you see a friend in the street but she completely ignores you, so you think that you must have done something to upset her. You don't know this—she might be in a hurry to get somewhere, or her mind might be on other things.

Jumping to conclusions also involves mind-reading (assuming you know what someone else is thinking) and crystal-ball-gazing (convincing yourself that you know how the future will turn out). In both cases, this is done on the basis of insufficient knowledge and, for someone affected by mental health problems, it usually involves the negative.

Magnification

Magnification is similar to over-generalisation in that it involves taking a single negative trait or event and blowing it out of all proportion. For example, on the basis of a single mistake you come to believe that you are "incompetent".

Emotional reasoning

Emotional reasoning involves interpreting the world according to how you feel. For example, someone makes a comment that upsets you so you form the belief that they meant to upset you. When out driving, someone does something that makes you feel angry, so you believe that they deliberately set out to make you angry.

Should/must/ought thoughts

The words should, must and ought are among the most abused (and abusive) in the English language because they describe ideals that real life simply can't live up to: "he should treat me better than this", "she ought to look after herself better", "I must stop doing that".

Underlying these thoughts is a (sometimes unconscious) "ideal-type" model of how you believe the world/life/you should be. For someone affected by mental illness, this model becomes a stick to beat themselves with every time life turns out to be different.

Personalisation and blame

While most of us live with the belief that we are in control of our lives and our destiny, the truth is that much is out of our control. For example, the economic crisis that shook the world in 2008 continues to result in people losing jobs, families and relationships breaking down and people becoming homeless. When you are caught up in these things, it can be difficult to see the wider picture. It is often easier to blame yourself or those around you.

For someone affected by mental illness, personalisation and blame means dismissing the wider picture and always seeing negative events as personal. This, in turn, results in a sense of guilt and a tendency to blame oneself for everything that goes wrong.

These forms of distorted thinking serve to compound mental distress because they impact on emotions and behaviours.

This can develop into a vicious circle in which each negative thought leads to deeper depression which leads to negative behaviour which leads to new negative thoughts. For example, someone thinks they will never get work. This makes them feel down, and results in them taking less care of their appearance, being more negative in their speech, and not applying for work as often as they might. When they do get invited for a job interview, their negative outlook and poor personal appearance works against them. When they do not get the job, this confirms their negative thought that they are "unemployable". And so it goes on…

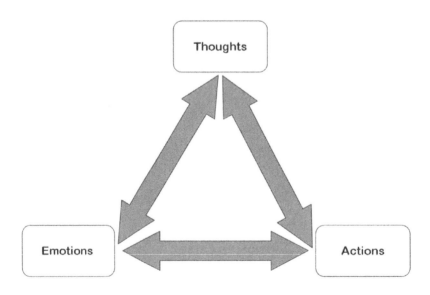

When helping someone who is experiencing mental distress, and using our model:

- o **Listen**
- o **Assess**
- o **Signpost to appropriate support**
- o **Self-help**.

Part of your listening will involve being alert to these thought distortions being expressed in what the person you are listening to is saying. Where someone is expressing lots of distorted thoughts, and where these are affecting them to a large degree, you should encourage them to seek professional support.

There is are many psychological or "talking" therapies that can help someone address distorted thinking. For example, Cognitive Behavioural Therapy (CBT) is designed to interrupt the spiral of negative thoughts, emotions and behaviours by encouraging the person to analyse their thoughts and beliefs, consider the (often lack of) evidence for them, and to substitute more helpful thoughts and beliefs.

Counselling and CBT are available through your family doctor (although there may be waiting lists). They may also be available through:

- o Local voluntary organisations (e.g., MIND: www.mind.org.uk)
- o Employers (via an Employee Assistance Programme)
- o Private medical insurance
- o Private practice.

This will vary from area to area.

There are also several computerised CBT packages available such as *Beating the Blues* (www.beatingtheblues.co.uk) which are available on prescription in many parts of the UK.

Work with core skills

Each of us has personal abilities and skills that, when harnessed, help give meaning to our lives. However, we often find that life thwarts us, leaving us in roles where we are obliged to do things that we are not good at or that we do not enjoy doing.

We see this quite often in service roles such as policing, teaching and nursing. People taking up these roles often have an aptitude for caring, supporting and encouraging people. However, the need to be publicly accountable means that people delivering these services spend an increasing proportion of their time conforming to "performance targets", form-filling, and "managing" their role rather than actually doing it.

People experiencing mental distress often find that their core skills and abilities are not fully utilised or are frustrated. Of course, symptoms of mental distress such as loss of memory and concentration can compound this. So too can the stigma and discrimination that result in people with diagnoses of mental illness being excluded from employment.

This is a key reason why volunteering is a popular route to recovery for many of those with diagnoses of mental illness. Volunteering offers the possibility of working to your core skills and abilities with less of the stigma that continues to beset employment (although so-called "third sector" organisations are not immune from discrimination either).

In practice, you can either exercise your core skills and abilities in your work or (much more commonly) you can use work as a means of funding you so that you can deploy your skills and abilities through hobbies and/or through voluntary work.

In the long-term, someone experiencing mental distress may want to think about whether they are in the right employment. A change of employment might be possible, or they may be able to re-train or go back into education in order to develop their skills and abilities and to obtain the qualifications required to make the change.

In the short-term, you can encourage them to stay engaged in activities, hobbies or volunteering roles that allow them to use and develop their core skills and abilities.

This will be particularly important if they are unemployed. Mental distress is usually accompanied by extreme tiredness coupled to a tendency to withdraw from society. When someone feels this low, it may feel comfortable to stay at home catching up on sleep or trying to relax in front of the TV. But this can quickly become a vicious downward spiral—the less they engage and the more they sleep during the day, the worse their mental distress becomes.

Re-engaging with things they are good at, that they used to enjoy doing, or that they had always wanted to try, can form a key part of getting them out of this downward spiral and back into social circulation. Also, engaging in activities that utilise their core skills and abilities will help them to overcome feelings of low self-esteem and self-worth—particularly if they are able to use these in a voluntary role that allows them to help and support other people.

Bringing Self-help Together

Personal wellbeing and resilience to mental distress involve bringing all of the elements of our being into line. Imagine one of those old combination locks that requires you to bring all of the wheels into line to unlock it. For optimal wellbeing we all need to align our:

o   Social being
o   Physical being
o   Emotional being
o   Mental being
o   Core skills and abilities.

When someone has all of these elements working together, they often experience a sense of "flowing" or what top sportsmen and women refer to as "being in the zone" - everything they are doing seems to work easily and seamlessly.

Unfortunately, few of us have this experience throughout our lives. Someone who is experiencing mental distress is likely to be experiencing problems in all areas, and may see the tasks involved in self-help as overwhelming. However, it is important that they are encouraged to do something.

Often, people feel drawn to one or other element of self-help. For example, one person might want to improve their diet while another will decide to be more physically active. It is important to encourage them to follow through with any activity or lifestyle change that they feel drawn to.

Remember that your role is to encourage, not to nag or coerce— there are dangers in pushing someone who is experiencing mental distress too hard.

Take small steps

Adopting a healthier lifestyle or taking up new activities can be daunting. It is all too easy to allow yourself to be put off. Someone who has mental distress must also battle against the inertia and limitations that come with mental illness.

It is easy for them to believe that the task is not worth starting because they do not believe they will ever finish it. Moreover, at the start, their mental health problems may lead them to feel exhausted and more unwell—particularly if they try to do too much too quickly.

The trick with mental health is to take everything in small manageable steps. This is rather like someone training to run a marathon. There is no point just arriving on the day. You have to train regularly for month after month to get to the point where you can do it.

With mental health, you have to start where the person you are helping is. If, for example, prolonged social withdrawal has led to agoraphobia, there is no point expecting them to go out shopping with you. However, you might encourage them to sit with you in the garden. And when they are comfortable with this, you might build up to walking along the street, then, perhaps, to using a local shop, etc. Taken gradually, they will get back to full social engagement. It is just a matter of time and patience.

Draw up a plan

Similarly, there is no point in encouraging someone to shop for fresh ingredients if they have not first learned how to store, prepare and cook them.

Adopting a healthy diet might require some thought and planning. For example, the first step might be to learn to cook. This could be by getting a friend or relative to show them how it is done. It could involve learning from a book, DVD or internet site. It could involve attending an adult learning class.

Buying healthy ingredients needs to be thought about. Do they want the convenience of buying everything in one go? Or would they prefer to shop around. Can they afford to buy whatever they want? Or do they need to get value for money? This will determine whether they shop at a single supermarket or whether they visit a range of different outlets.

The danger for someone with mental health problems is that they will "do it tomorrow". But tomorrow never comes. Writing a plan can help them stay on track, and it can help you to keep them motivated. If they agree to do something, you can check whether they have, and if not, why not?

Remember to work at their pace. If they are very poorly and cannot do much, something as simple as doing some things around the house can be planned. Indeed, done properly, this can help provide a sense of achievement.

Saying, "I will clean the house" is unlikely to work. But setting out a plan allows the task to be broken into achievable chunks. For example:

Monday:

10.30—pick up clutter in the living room

11.00—put rubbish in the bin

12.00—vacuum the living room

14.00—pick up clothes from bedroom

14.30—load washing machine

These can be ticked off as they are achieved:

10.30—pick up clutter in the living room ✓

11.00—put rubbish in the bin ✓

12.00—vacuum the living room ✗

14.00—pick up clothes from bedroom ✓

14.30—load washing machine ✓

In this way, they can see the things they have done rather than focusing on the things they have not. Also, they can be more aware of any problems they may have had. For example (remembering that someone with mental health problems can quickly become tired) they may have been unable to do the vacuuming because they had overdone things earlier, and may have needed to rest. Knowing this means they can scale down the things they plan to do next time.

This process of planning and breaking activities down into small manageable chunks can be applied to anything they want to achieve.

Keep a diary

Along with any plans they make, it can help to encourage them to keep a record of health-promoting activities that they engage in every day. Over time, this can help them understand how some things make them feel better and some things make them feel worse.

Keeping a diary will allow them to check their mood and energy levels against:

o   The amount of sleep they are getting

o   The amount of physical activity they do

o   Their diet (based on 5-a-day)

o   Their fluid intake (6-glasses-a-day)

o   Their alcohol intake

o   Any other quick-fixes

o   And their daily achievements.

Keeping a daily record in this way will help them identify the things that they are doing which improve their wellbeing as well as those that make matters worse. This may not be obvious without keeping a record. For example, looking back through the record you may find that someone who over-uses alcohol on Friday and Saturday goes on to experience low mood and energy levels on Monday and Tuesday. Similarly, someone may try doing exercise on Monday and claim that it leaves them feeling tired. But checking the record may show that in weeks when they did exercise on a Monday, their mood and energy levels were much improved on Tuesday and Wednesday.

Look After Yourself

Helping someone who has mental health problems can be a wearing process, particularly if your relationship to them means that you are going to be in for the long-term.

It is all too easy to let their needs take priority over yours. This opens you to the risk of prolonged stress and burn out. Remember that if you get ill, you will not be able to help them anyway. So set some boundaries and stick to them.

You can't do it for them

People affected by mental health problems will often seek a quick-fix or magic wand to take away their problems. However, the solution is almost always a gradual process of lifestyle changes coupled to problem solving that will gradually return them to health and wellbeing.

While it may seem like a kindness for you to do things for them, this is likely to stand in the way of their recovery in the longer-term. It is better if you take the role of a mentor—encouraging them to do things for themselves—as ultimately, this is the only way they are going to recover and learn to manage their problems in future.

Don't let them "test" your commitment

It is common for people affected by mental health problems to try to test your love, loyalty and devotion by saying and doing things that are upsetting, or that seem to be intended to drive you away.

Again, the way to avoid this problem is to set out your boundaries from the beginning. Let them know that you are there to help, but that they must take responsibility for themselves.

If and when they say or do things that seem designed to push you away, gently but firmly remind them of the rules.

Keep an eye on your stress levels

Remember that the things we do to unwind in the wake of short-term stress are also the things we turn to when stress is on-going. If, for example, you like a glass of wine as a way of unwinding after work, you may find that as your stress levels increase, so too does your wine consumption. Similarly, a chocaholic will find their chocolate consumption increasing as their stress levels go up. While these ways of coping are relatively harmless in the short-term, they can take a toll on your health with prolonged use.

Take time for yourself

Helping someone else can mean letting go of some of the things that you enjoy and that help to keep you happy and healthy. It may be tempting to sacrifice more than is healthy in the hope that the person you are helping will make a quick recovery. However, helping with mental health problems is often a long haul. So you are better pacing yourself.

Taking time to do the things for yourself and spending time with people whose company you enjoy may seem selfish when someone you care about is poorly. However, if you do not do them, the end result is that you will also become stressed, and may even develop mental health problems of your own!

Set aside time to relax

A simple but important way of coping with stress is to take time out to really relax. This need only take 20 minutes out of a busy day, but it is important that you set time aside and stick to it. If you can, get into a routine. Same place same time every day.

If you have difficulty relaxing, you could try using a relaxation CD. You might try a relaxation class or a complementary therapy. You might find that doing some physical exercise prior to relaxation is particularly effective—this is why many people attend yoga classes.

Talk, talk and more talk...

Just as when someone has problems, the best thing you can do for them is to listen, so when your stress levels are high, the best thing you can do is find someone to listen to you.

This might not need to be as formal as would be the case when you are helping someone who has a mental health problem. Nevertheless, finding time to talk to friends or relatives can help you return your stress levels to normal.

Talking on the phone or arranging to meet up for a chat is the easiest way of dealing with stress.

If you feel that there is nobody to talk to, or that you do not want people to know about the person you have been helping, you could use a helpline—there are several public helplines (see chapter 6 on useful resources). Alternatively, if you are employed, you may have access to a counselling helpline through an Employee Assistance Programme. Helplines are usually confidential, so there is no risk of anything you say getting back to anyone you know.

If you have particular problems, you could look at getting face-to-face counselling.

Ask for help

Don't feel that you have to do everything yourself. It serves nobody's interest for you to get so stressed that your wellbeing suffers.

It is important that your help and encouragement is not the only thing that the person you are helping is relying on. It is important that they are accessing the help that is available from the NHS, voluntary groups and their employer (if need be, you can talk to these service providers directly to see what support they can give). And it is essential that they help themselves.

Carers organisations can also be a useful resource for you. Although these are generalist organisations, they provide a wealth of information about the types of support that are available to anyone who is caring for someone else.

Useful Resources

Although this book has presented the basic information about mental health problems and mental illness that a lay-helper needs to know, there is a vast amount of information and advice available for people who want to go into this in more depth.

Official information

The two official sources of information that provide a starting point for finding information and support are:

o   NHS Choices (www.nhs.uk) which provides information and access to further support on most illnesses, including mental illness. The site also offers further information on self-help.
o   Direct Gov (www.direct.gov.uk) is a gateway to the full range of UK public services, and also provides links out to other support organisations.

You might also want to visit the health pages on the BBC and Channel 4 websites.

Charities

There are thousands of charities around the UK that provide information and support to people with mental illness and mental health problems. There are hundreds of thousands that run activities that are of benefit too. The best way of finding these is through your local Association of Voluntary Organisations.

The main national mental health charities are:

o   **Mind** (www.mind.org.uk) (0300 123 3393)which is a national campaigning body that franchises its brand to hundreds of local charities throughout the UK (you will find your nearest branch through their website).

o **Rethink** (www.rethink.org) (0300 5000 927) Formerly the National Schizophrenia Fellowship, Rethink has tended to focus on supporting people with severe mental illness. However, their website also contains information about common conditions such as anxiety and depression.

o **Bipolar UK** (www.bipolaruk.org.uk) (020 7931 6480) focuses on supporting people with bipolar depression (aka manic depression). You can find information and links to their national network of self-help groups on the site.

o **Depression Alliance** (www.depressionalliance.org) provides information about depression together with links to their network of UK self-help groups.

o **Anxiety UK** (www.anxietyuk.org.uk) (08444774) provides information about anxiety, and operates a network of groups around the UK.

o **Campaign Against Living Miserably** (CALM) (www.thecalmzone.net) provides information and support to young men aged 15-35.

o **Mental Health Foundation** (www.mentalhealth.org.uk) carries out research into mental illness, and provides information and publications about mental health issues.

o **Papyrus** (www.papyrus-uk.org) (0800 068 4141) provides specialist support to people helping children and young people who are at risk of suicide.

o **Alcoholics Anonymous** (www.alcoholics-anonymous.org.uk) (0845 769 7555) **Narcotics Anonymous** (www.ukna.org) (0300 999 1212) and **Gamblers Anonymous** (www.gamblersanonymous.org.uk) provide information and support to people with those addictions.

- **Cruse Bereavement Care** (www.crusebereavementcare.org.uk) (0844 477 9400) offers advice, information and support to people who have experienced the loss of a loved one. They also operate a large network of local branches throughout the UK.
- **BEAT** (www.b-eat.co.uk) provides specialist advice, information and support to people affected by eating disorders. They also operate a network of support services throughout the UK.
- **No Panic** (www.nopanic.org.uk) provides information and support to people affected by panic attacks, panic disorders and OCD.

Carers charities

- **Carers UK** (www.carersuk.org) are a campaigning organisation who offer information, advice and support to carers. Their site also has a forum where you can communicate with other carers.
- **The Carers Trust** (www.carers.org) offers information advice and support, and runs a network of local carers groups across the UK.

Helplines

Some of the charities listed above operate helplines. In addition, you could call:

- Community Advice and Listening Line (CALL): 0800 123 737
- Sane: 0845 767 8000
- Samaritans: 08457 90 90 90
- Young Minds (for parents): 0808 802 5544.

About Life Surfing

Life Surfing is a not-for-profit Community Interest Company that was established to provide a coaching, mentoring and training approach for people experiencing common life problems that can cause stress, anxiety and depression.

Our mission is to help people learn to cope with life without the need to call on over-stretched NHS services that are better deployed to help people with severe mental illness.

Over the years we have found that there is a huge amount that people can do to develop their personal resources and to foster their own wellbeing. In most cases, the real need is for encouragement, support, knowledge and skills.

This is what Life Surfing offers.

We have developed a range of services – one-to-one coaching, training workshops, mentoring groups and a range of publications - to give you the knowledge, skills and motivation needed to address life's issues and overcome stress-related problems in a healthy way, and to promote your long-term personal wellbeing.

For further information, please visit the Life Surfing website:

www.life-surfing.com
info@life-surfing.com

Or you can contact us on: 0300 321 4514 / 07922 537 646

Box 124, R&R Consulting Centre
41 St. Isan Road
Heath Cardiff CF14 4LW

Printed in Great Britain
by Amazon